AF494947

CONVIVENCIA AND ITS FRENCH AND ENGLISH EQUIVALENTS

Dominique-D Junod (Arbell)

Convivencia and its French and English equivalents

The word and the concept

(Online research)

Translated by Martin Hemmings

Editions Florent HUET

ISBN 979-10-91662-21-5

Foreword

Convivencia, convivance, « convivence »

Executive summary

Convivencia is a well-known, long-established and widely used word, particularly in Spain and France. The French version of the word, *convivance,* was formally accepted for inclusion in the thesaurus of the Académie Française in 2004. The English word "convivence", meanwhile, is gaining ground in the United Kingdom and is already widely used in the United States. The word can also be found in a number of other languages, such as Catalan, Occitan, Portuguese and Italian (a slightly different word, *ta'ayuch* (coexistence) is used in Arabic).

The word *convivencia* (and its equivalents *convivance* and "convivence") comes from the Latin "*cum vivere*". In all languages that use the word, its meaning is the same: the ability to live with others and to live together in the same space. Historians often use the word in reference to the social and legal practices introduced by Muslims following their conquest of the Iberian Peninsula (and the establishment of Córdoba as their capital city in the 8th century) and their subsequent occupation of other regions.

From the establishment of the first Emirate of Córdoba, and throughout the third Umayyad Caliphate, Córdoba's Christian and Jewish communities were classed as protected subjects (*dhimmis)* by their Muslim conquerors and were allowed to practise their own religious beliefs, commercial activities and scientific research freely. The most brilliant minds of the age were able to express their talents in all walks of life – from art and religion to healthcare and medicine – regardless of their religious persuasion. Indeed, some of their works remain important influences to this day.

The word *convivencia* is now used in a slightly different way than in the past. Once a word to express the now legendary harmony that existed in Córdoba and radiated across Al-Andalus, *convivencia*, *convivance*, or "convivence," is now used with reference to any practice, method or action undertaken to promote and encourage harmonious coexistence between individuals and communities in all walks of private, social and political life.

Examples of *convivencia* can therefore be found in couples and families, between housemates, and between religious, social or cultural communities living in the same neighbourhood, city, region, country or continent.

The word *convivencia* is associated with words such as tolerance, friendship, cohabitation, coexistence and harmony. However, it is in fact a much broader concept that includes, but is not directly equivalent to, these notions.

Dominique-D Junod (Arbell)
PhD Political Sciences. BA Ancient and Modern Studies. University of Geneva.
November 2011

Contents

Introduction

The word *convivencia* is often used in Spanish, French and English – especially by historians – to refer to the relatively harmonious coexistence (allowing for temporal and circumstantial fluctuations) between Christian, Jewish and Muslim communities during the Muslim conquest of the Iberian Peninsula and Septimania to the north, prior to the "Reconquista" (711-1492). This region, and the civilisation that developed there, were known as "Al-Andalus" and its capital was at Córdoba. This peaceful coexistence between different religious communities was a key feature of the Emirate of Córdoba, and the subsequent Caliphate of Córdoba, based on teachings from the Qur'an. Non-Muslims – mostly Jews and Christians – were invited or even forced to accept "protected subject" status (dhimmis), covering their religious, cultural and economic practices.

The peaceful coexistence between residents from different communities (i.e. their *convivencia*) was not without its own difficulties, and has been the subject of much debate among historians. What remains certain, however, is that this arrangement produced remarkably effective intercultural and economic results, with major religious, artistic, medical and economic works from all three communities continuing to have an influence to this day. This initial model of *convivencia*, as established in Córdoba, was then and remains today a key contribution to the history of humanity, notwithstanding the inevitable disagreements, rivalries and conflicts between communities. [1]

These days, this "Golden Age" of *convivencia* – now seen by many as a legendary and somewhat "blessed" period of history – is often referred to in connection with successful dialogue or action that results in peaceful coexistence between individuals or groups, where the parties concerned have a desire to live together in harmony while respecting each other's differences. [2]

In this study, we will look at the words *convivencia* in Spanish (and Catalan), *convivance* in French (*convivencia* in Occitan) and "convivence" in English, as well as the concept underlying this term. We will adopt a different approach for each language concerned, as the word has its own specific connotations

---

[1] A more detailed account can be found in *Convivencia, Jews, Muslims and Christians in Medieval Spain* Edited by Vivan B. Mann, Thomas F. Glick and Jerrilynn D. Dodds, George Braziller in association with The Jewish Museum, New York, (1992)

[2] For those unfamiliar with the history of the Al-Andalus period, more details can be found in Angelo Hüsler's book, *L'Espagne médiévale, Chrétiens Juifs et Musulmans*, Infolio, 2008 (available in French only), which gives a clear and simple account of the history of Al-Andalus from 711 to 1492 and explains how Muslims, Jews and Christians lived together under the Caliphate of Córdoba. Hüsler, who is Swiss, uses the French word "*co-existence*".

and evolution in each, thereby demanding a differentiated research and questioning strategy. In this small-scale research project, conducted online, we will also suggest areas of further research and consideration. This is a research topic that certainly merits further development, and the conclusions drawn herein are purely indicative in nature.

I. *Convivencia*: the word and the concept in ancient times

The word comes from the Latin *cum vivere* – which translates literally as "to live with".[3] All sources consulted agree on this point.

When did the word *convivencia* appear and was it used in the Al-Andalus period or in ancient times? According to philologist and historian Ramón Menéndez Pidal, the word existed at the time of the Medieval Iberian Peninsula. [4]

When attempting to ascertain the origins of the word *convivencia*, it is important to put the situation in which it emerged in context. Al-Andalus covered not only the territory occupied by modern-day Spain, but also other regions to the north, including Septimania, now part of Occitania in southern France, where the Oc language (and related dialects) are still spoken to this day. There was naturally significant interaction between the languages spoken by the Andalusian Arab and Iberian populations (from Catalonia), and the emerging Oc language in the southern regions of France. [5] Indeed, there is evidence that Occitan troubadours from the 12th century onwards used

---

3 http://www.elalmanaque.com/lexico/convivencia.htm

4 Ramón Menéndez Pidal, *Orígenes del español*, 1926.

5 http://www.convivance-liens.com/Mona/articles.php?lng=fr&pg=104

to sing about the harmonious coexistence that was a key feature of life in Al-Andalus. However, in these regions, the word *convivencia* was not yet used. Instead, they talked of *paratge* (denoting equality and honour).[6]

The word *convivencia* did not appear in Occitania until later. The exact date, however, is unknown. In his 1965 book entitled *Le 'Joy d'Amor' des troubadours,*[7] Charles Camproux[8], an Occitan-French author, uses the word, borrowing it from modern Catalan. According to Camproux, the term has also been "adopté par les autres dialectes d'Oc cultivés d'aujourd'hui" [adopted by other modern-day Occitan dialects] and, in his estimation, it is "essentiellement indiqué pour désigner un des caractères essentiels, sinon le caractère essentiel, de la civilisation dont naturellement se nourrissait le XII° siècle des troubadours" [primarily used to refer to one of –

[6] Reference unclear. However, I received this information in a personal email from Professor Alem Surre Garcia on 17 August 2012.

[7] Charles Camproux, *Le 'Joy d'Amor' des troubadours, Jeu et Joie d'amour*, Montpellier, Cause, Castelnau, 1965.

[8] Charles Camproux (1908-1994) is a key figure in modern Occitan culture. He played a major role in the birth of modern Occitanism in the inter-war period and introduced Occitan studies at university level. His linguistic works represent a major contribution to our understanding of the Occitan language. http://occitanica.eu/omeka/items/show/378 [English translation]

if not THE – essential characteristics of the civilisation from which 12th century troubadours drew their inspiration].[9] He does not refer directly to Al-Andalus, but talks more generally of a civilisation of *convivencia*, which he defines as "ce sens aigu de la liberté qui entraine comme conséquence le sens d'une très large tolérance" [a sense of great freedom which, in turn, gives rise a sense of great tolerance].[10]

Professor Alem Surre-Garcia[11] sets up a direct relationship between Al-Andalus, *convivencia* and the

---

[9] Citation with unclear reference in an email from Alem Surre-Garcia to Dominique Arbell on 17 August 2012.

[10] According to a description of the book in the journal *Cahiers de civilisation médiévale*, 1966, vol. 9, p. 568, cited at http://www.persee.fr/web/revues/home/prescript/article/ccmed_0007-9731_1966_num_9_36_1396_t1_0568_0000_1

[11] Alem Surre-Garcia was born in 1944 near Toulouse and is of Galician descent. He was head of culture for the Conseil Régional de Midi-Pyrénées (Midi-Pyrénées Regional Council) between 1989 and 2006. He is an Occitan writer whose works have been translated into many languages, including German, French, Polish and Catalan. He also translates works by major Occitan writers into French. He is a librettist, playwright, lecturer, cultural event organiser and French-language essay writer. http://www.editions-harmattan.fr/index.asp?navig=auteurs&obj=artiste&no=18962. He is the author of *Au-delà des Rives, les Orients*

material from which the troubadours drew their inspiration. He argues that the concept of *convivencia* in Occitania "vient de l'Espagne andalouse où chrétiens, juifs et musulmans inventaient un équilibre où chacun pouvait s'épanouir. Le modèle remonte ensuite vers le nord, le mot occitan "*convivencia*" apparaît et (faut-il comprendre "tandis que" ?") les troubadours diffusent cet art de vivre ensemble dans le respect des différences en termes d'égalité." [comes from Spain during the Al-Andalus period, when Christians, Jews and Muslims established a balanced system under which everyone was able to flourish. The model then moved northwards, the Occitan word *convivencia* appeared and (or indeed "while"?) the troubadours sang about this harmonious coexistence and mutual respect for difference in terms of equality].[12]

The Spanish word *convivencia,* as transposed into Occitan, is therefore an integral part of the "histoire du pourtour méditerranéen occitan qui voyait cohabiter pacifiquement les juifs séfarades d'Espagne, les musulmans (arabo andalous) occupant la Septimanie (Languedoc Roussillon actuel) et la Provence, et les Wisigoths bâtisseurs de Toulouse (Tolosa). Tout ce petit

---

d'Occitanie . De la fondation de Marseille à l'expulsion des juifs du Royaume de France. 316 pages, Dervy, 2 May 2005.

[12] http://www.la-croix.com/Actualite/S-informer/France/La-convivencia-methode-occitane-pour-accepter-ses-differences-_EP_-2012-02-01-764546

monde commerçait habilement, Narbonne rayonnait autant que Byzance et on se mariait entre communautés pour souder les alliances" [history of the Occitan Mediterranean region, where Sephardic Jews from Spain, Andalusian Arab Muslims living in Septimania (modern-day Languedoc Roussillon] and Provence and the Visigoths who built Toulouse (Tolosa) lived together in peace. Through clever business transactions, Narbonne became as important a trade centre as Byzantium, and members of different communities inter-married to build alliances].[13]

Were the word and the underlying concept retained by the Castilians (Toledo School of Translators), the Catalonians and the Jews expelled from Grenada in 1492, who continued to use their own form of Spanish (Judaeo-Spanish or Ladino), and whose name, "Sephardic", means "Spanish"?[14]

---

13 http://www.convivance-liens.com/Mona/articles.php?lng=fr&pg=104 - Also see Alem Surre- Garcia, *Au-delà des Rives, les Orients d'Occitanie. De la fondation de Marseille à l'expulsion des juifs du Royaume de France.* 316 pages, Dervy, 2 May 2005.

14 Eli Tauber, El idioma judéo espanol en Bosnia Herzegovina, editado por la *El idioma judeoespañol en Bosnia-Herzegovin*a fue editado por La Benevolencia, asociación ultural y humanitaria judía de Bosnia - señaló que su libro desea mostrar "con cuánto amor los sefardíes

The Real Academia Española is currently working on a *Diccionario historico* (historical dictionary) which may shed some light on these questions.[15] This vast dictionary will, in effect, be a glossary of ancient terms, which should provide a vital resource for interpreting ancient Spanish texts.

---

han guardado y preservado ese español medieval, el lenguaje de Cervantes."

[15] http://lema.rae.es/drae/

II. *Convivencia* in modern Spanish

Historian Americo Castro[16], in a book published in 1948 (no longer available in Spanish for now)[17] and translated into English,[18] was seemingly the first modern author to turn his attentions to an analysis of *convivencia.* Other authors then followed suit, and *convivencia* became the subject of wide debate. In a conference paper entitled "Al Andalus, 800 años de convivencia", Professor

---

[16] http://es.wikipedia.org/wiki/Américo_Castro. Partial biography: Américo Castro nació en Cantagalo (Brasil) de parents originaires de Granada. (…) Se graduó en la Universidad de Granada en 1904, en Letras y Derecho, e hizo el doctorado en Madrid. Luego pasó a Francia para estudiar en la Sorbona (1905-07) y, al quedar huérfano, tuvo que sustentarse dando clases de español en París. Estudió también en Alemania, pero volvió a Madrid y comenzó a colaborar con Ramón Menéndez Pidal en el Centro de Estudios Históricos, así como con la Institución Libre de Enseñanza, con cuyo grupo estaba relacionado. En 1910 ayudó a organizar el Centro de Estudios Históricos en Madrid, sirviendo como jefe del departamento de lexicografía; luego seguiría vinculado a esta institución incluso después de que se convirtiera en catedrático de Historia de la Lengua Española en la universidad madrileña en 1915.

[17] Castro, Américo, *Espana en su historica, cristianos, moros y judios* . Buenos Aires, Editorial Losada. First edition: 1948.

[18] English translation: Castro, Américo, The Spaniards, An Introduction to their history. Enlarged by three chapters, Berkeley, University of California Press. 1971.

Shamsuddin Elia[19], offers a brief and clear overview of the achievements of the Al-Andalus civilisation, focusing in particular on the concept of *convivencia.* In a section entitled "Convivencia y Tolerancia", he argues that the lasting legacy of Spain's Muslim civilisation was its undeniable spirit of tolerance.[20]

---

[19] A practising Sunni Muslim living in Buenos Aires

[20] Conference paper by Professor Shamsuddin Elia : *El Islam: arte, derecho, economía, filosofía, historia y teología. 15 siglos de civilización y cultura,"* que tuvo lugar en Buenos Aires, en la Facultad de Derecho de la Universidad Nacional de Lomas de Zamora, del 23 de Octubre al 27 de Noviembre de 1.996. http://www.arabespanol.org/andalus/800ano.htm '« lo que mejor caracteriza el legado hispano-musulmán es su espíritu de la tolerancia. Si hablamos de la tolerancia del Islam, no se trata de un tópico repetido con fines propagandísticos, sino de una experiencia y una realidad histórica irrefutable. En la llamada Edad de Oro del Islam, cuando el territorio musulmán se extendía de España hasta la China, entre los siglos VIII y XIV, convivían en su seno en un ambiente de libertad y mutuo respeto cristianos arrianos, nestorianos, monofisitas y coptos, judíos, budistas, zoroastrianos, maniquéos e hinduistas, cuyas creencias y tradiciones eran garantizadas por el Islam por el estatuto de *Ahl al Dhimma,* es decir, la "Gente del Pacto". Esto es algo que el Islam puso en práctica hace más de 1.400 años y que Occidente a duras

Despite differing opinions on the history of *convivencia*[21], the "idealism" of *convivencia* has gradually taken root in the Spanish consciousness and in the modern Spanish language. The word *convivencia* can be found in the 2001 edition of the dictionary of the Real Academia Española, the Spanish equivalent of France's Académie Française. It defines *convivencia* simply as the "acción de convivir" (act of living together). [22] The word *convivencia* also has an entry in the 1998 edition of the Larousse Spanish-French bilingual dictionary, and is linked to the French words "vie en commun" (living together), "cohabitation" (cohabitation) and "coexistence" (coexistence).[23]

The citations below provide an overview of what the word *convivencia* means to modern-day Spaniards:

- Couple psychology:

---

penas comenzó a llevarlo a cabo a mediados del siglo XX."

[21] Arielle Erin Golden, Convivencia and Conversos, Problematizing Identity, PhD thesis, CNN Wesleyan University, Connecticut, 2010. Viewable online. http://wesscholar.wesleyan.edu

[22] http://lema.rae.es/drae/?val=convivencia. 1.f.

[23] I did not conduct any systematic or reverse research in dictionaries.

"Sabemos que no es fácil convivir con alguien, cualquiera sea la relación quenos una, con mayor razón la *convivencia* en pareja puede resultar aún más compleja."[24]

- Sociology (family unit):

"Una de las formas más usuales en que se verifica la *convivencia* es la familia, unidad básica de la vida social o comunitaria. "[25]

- Citizenship:

" ... el término "*convivencia*", al menos en castellano, tiene connotaciones de una mayor exigencia que la simple coexistencia. Coexistir sólo exige que quienes coexisten se mantengan en la existencia al mismo tiempo, sin importar en qué condiciones, más o menos hostiles, ocurra tal hecho. En cambio, convivir exige la realización práctica de ciertos compromisos en cuanto a respeto mutuo, a cooperación voluntaria y a compartir responsabilidades. "[26]

- Formal education:

---

[24] http://psicologia.laguia2000.com/el-amor/la-convivencia-en-pareja

[25] http://es.wikipedia.org/wiki/Convivencia#Bibliograf.C3.ADa

[26] Enciclopedia de Paz y de Conflictos. http://www.educacionparalapaz.org.co/enciclopedia/concep_9/concepto10.htm

" El presente documento constituye una primera aproximación para la formulación, en términos teóricos, conceptuales y operacionales, de una forma de pedagogía destinada a dar respuesta al gran problema que representa hoy la convivencia en la escuela. Tentativamente incorpora la expresión *pedagogía de la convivencia*, para dar cuenta de este esfuerzo. "[27]

- Art and culture:

20minutos.es, a Spanish news website, "muestran la *convivencia* artística de cristianos, musulmanes y judíos en el Imperio Bizantino" dans le cadre de "La gran exposición 'Bizancio y el Islam, una era de transición' reúne en el MET de Nueva York 300 obras derivadas de la colaboración entre las tres culturas."[28]

- Social sciences:

---

[27] Article 'Hacia una Pedagogía de la Convivencia'. Roberto Arístegui, Domingo Bazán, Jorge Leiva, Ricardo López, Bernardo Muñoz y Juan Ruz. *Organización de Estados Iberoamericanos* (OEI), *PSYKHE 2005*, Vol. 14, N° 1, 137 – 150. http://www.scielo.cl/scielo.php?pid=S0718-22282005000100011&script=sci_arttext

[28] http://www.20minutos.es/noticia/1330482/0/convivencia/cristianos-musulmanes-judios/imperio-bizantino/

" En este trabajo vamos a abordar un tema muy amplio como es la *convivencia* que intentaremos concretar, dirigiéndolo hacia un aspecto que nos interesa en nuestra labor como docentes : el diálogo. "[29]

- Spanish and European politics:

Description of the content of a work on the Spanish constitution and its importance in terms of Europe:

"La Constitución española en el contexto constitucional europeo es un análisis de 111 autores extranjeros que ubican nuestra Carta Magna dentro de un entorno más amplio: Europa. Presentada por la presidenta del Parlamento, Luisa Fernanda Rudi, el ministro de Defensa, Federico Trillo, y el representante del PSOE, Diego López Garrido los tres defendieron la Carta Magna como instrumento "indispensable" de *convivencia*"[30]

- Intercultural dialogue:

"El término de interculturalidad se refiere a la interacción entre culturas, donde se concibe que ningún grupo cultural está por encima del otro, favoreciendo en

---

[29] 'La convivencia y el diálogo: ¿sabemos hablar y escuchar?' Cristina Palacios de Torres. *Revue Contribuciones a las ciencas sociales, 2009.* http://www.eumed.net/rev/cccss/index.htm.

[30] http://www.elmundo.es/documentos/2003/12/espana/constitucion/libros.html

todo momento la integración y *convivencia* de ambas partes."[31]

The word *convivencia* is also used in reference to the fight against terrorism. On Monday 7 April 2008, the Manuel Broseta Foundation awarded a "Convivencia" prize to French President Nicolas Sarkozy at the Élysée Palace.[32] The prize had been awarded to Spain's King Juan Carlos the previous year. The "Convivencia" prize was created in 1992 following the assassination of Professor Manuel Broseta by ETA in Valencia. It is awarded annually in recognition of efforts to defend freedom and liberty.

Convivencia is also used in the modern-day Catalan language:

In an English book defending the role of the Catalan language in Spain (with the support of Unesco), the author calls for "*convivencia*" between Castilian and Catalan, suggesting that the way in which the word *convivencia* is used in Catalan goes beyond simple cohabitation, referring instead to a method of living

---

[31] Nuria Otero Martínez, *Aprendiendo a vivir entre culturas, Cuadernos de Educación y de Desarrollo.* Vol 1. No 3. May 2009. http://www.eumed.net/rev/ced/03/nom.htm

[32] http://ambafrance-es.org/france_espagne/spip.php?article2731

together constructively and harmoniously in a spirit of friendship.[33]

The evidence given above clearly demonstrates that the spirit of *convivencia* (and its modern extensions) – which has its roots in Córdoba, the capital of *convivencia* – continues to resonate through Spain to this day. In modern Spain, the word *convivencia* and its underlying concept form an integral part of popular culture.

---

[33] Jacqueline Hall. *Convivencia in Catalonia: Languages living together*. 121 pages. Published by Fundacio Jaume Bofill. November 2001. ISBN 84-85557-55-7. Introduction page 15

III. The equivalent of *convivencia* in modern French: *convivance*

In modern French, the word *convivencia* has been "gallicised", becoming *convivance* (or *convivence* according to some authors).

The official spelling is *convivance,* the term having been included in the thesaurus of the Académie Française in autumn 2004.[34] According to Florence Delay[35], a member of the Académie Française, "une charte établie par l'association 'Pro Europae Unitatae', la

---

[34] Une très vieille convivance. *Séance publique annuelle des Cinq Académies*. 26 October 2004, by Mrs. Florence Delay. See the full text (in French only) on the Académie Française's website: http://www.academie-francaise.fr/node/3098

[35] Florence Delay is an eminent writer and academic, translator, and author of novels and essays. She is the daughter of Jean Delay, psychiatrist and member of the Académie Française, and the sister of Claude Delay, biographer and psychoanalyst. She is also a dramatist and playwright. Her academic works focus on romantic literature, Spanish and Medieval Spain, among other topics. She has worked with Jacques Roubaud, an academic specialising in poetry, verse and Medieval studies, and author of a bilingual anthology entitled *Les Troubadours.* Both Jacques Roubaud and Florence Delay have received numerous awards and prizes. These include the Grand Prix de Littérature Paul Morand, which he was awarded by the Académie Française in 2008.

'Charte européenne de la Convivance', avait eu premièrement recours à ce 'néologisme'" [a charter written by an association known as 'Pro Europae Unitatae', called the 'Charte européenne de la Convivance', was the first time that this 'neologism' was used]. In a letter of April 1995 to the permanent secretary of the Académie Française, its president argued that French journalists had been unable to translate the Pope's call for peace and dialogue during his 'Urbi et Orbi' papal address[36], delivered in Italian. On two separate occasions, John Paul II had called for "*convivenza*" between communities and between sections of individual communities. In their reports, several French journalists translated the word as "convivialité" (conviviality).[37] Similarly, many translators from across Europe, and particularly from Spain,

---

[36] *Messagio Urbi et Orbi di Sua Santità Giovanni Paolo II*, Domenica di Pascua, 16 April 1995: In this message, the Roman Catholic Church called on all peoples affected by conflict to choose dialogue as the only possible path to "convivenza" (convivencia in Italian), based on respect for others and mutual acceptance: "propone il dialogo come unica via atta a promuovere soluzioni eque, per una convivenza improntata al rispetto ed all'accoglienza réciproqua."

[37] Une très vieille convivance. *Séance publique annuelle des Cinq Académies*. 26 October 2004, by Mrs. Florence Delay. See the full text (in French only) on the Académie Française's website: http://www.academie-francaise.fr/node/3098

contacted the Académie Française to ask for the French equivalent of the word *convivenza.* [38]

Florence Delay made an impassioned speech in support of "*convivance*" to the members of the Institut de France in 2004: " (...) ce mot nouveau, pour moi, était très vieux. Il résonnait dans ma tête sous sa forme espagnole de *convivencia.* La *convivencia*? Ceux qui connaissent l'histoire de l'Espagne savent que ce mot embrasse une période qui dura près de huit siècles et pendant laquelle juifs, chrétiens et musulmans vécurent ensemble - de 711, où la péninsule hispanique fut conquise par quelques dizaines de milliers d'Arabes et de Berbères, à 1492, qui marque la fin de ce qu'on appelle la Reconquête. " [(...) this new word is in fact, in my estimation, an ancient word. In my mind, it is synonymous with its Spanish form, *convivencia.* What exactly is *convivencia*? Anyone with an understanding of the history of Spain will know that this word encompasses a period of almost eight centuries, during which Jews, Christians and Muslims lived peacefully side by side, from 711 when the Iberian Peninsula was conquered by tens of thousands of Arabs and Berbers, to 1492 at the end of the period known as the Reconquista.][39]

---

[38] Telephone interview between Florence Delay and Dominique Arbell, 11 October 2012.

[39] Une très vieille convivance. *Séance publique annuelle ...des Cinq Académies.* 26 October 2004, by Mrs. Florence Delay.

This speech has a strong "idealistic" undercurrent.[40] In Florence Delay's own words, it was "un appel à faire aussi bien de nos jours que du temps de Cordoue,[41] dans un contexte de "discordance" entre les trois religions. [an appeal to do today what was done in Córdoba, in response to "dissonance" between three religions.][42]

Why did the Académie Française decide to spell the word "*convivance*" rather than "*convivence*"?

Both spellings can be found both on the internet and in written publications. The Wiktionary website (a bilingual French and English dictionary), for example, spells the word with the ending "**-ence**"[43]:

convivence /kɔ̃.vi.vɑ̃s/ *féminin*

1. Fait, action de vivre ensemble pour des personnes ou pour des groupes de personnes :

Vie en société.

1. C'est pourquoi l'idée de la santé s'éleva à une importance religieuse par son origine, à une importance civile par la nécessite de procurer le bien-être physique à

---

[40] In a message from Florence Delay to Dominique Arbell via Isabelle Noel, Académie Française, 11 October 2012.

[41] Idem.

[42] Telephone interview between Florence Delay and Dominique Arbell, 11 October 2012.

[43] http://fr.wiktionary.org/wiki/convivence

la ***convivence*** *sociale.* — (Felix Henri Ranse, Marcel Baudouin, Jules René Guerin, *Gazette médicale de Paris*, Volume 24, 1853)

2. *(Spécialement)* Situation où cohabitent sur un même territoire, dans un même pays :

Mais le bilinguisme est le fruit soit de la naissance, donc de l'éducation, soit de la ***convivence*** *prolongée, soit d'un apprentissage volontaire et difficile.* — (Dennis Philips, *L'anglais : troisième langue de la Martinique ?* Centre d'étude et de recherche sur l'anglais langue étrangère aux Caraïbes, 1994.)"

In the French version of an official document on the development of language policies in Europe[44], published prior to the Académie Française's decision, the spelling "*convivence*" is also used. While strongly encouraging multilingualism, the document also warns decision-makers against the possible obstacle of "la question de l'incivilité, laquelle rejoint celle de la formation des citoyens aux valeurs collectives de la *convivence* démocratique." [the question of incivility,

[44] *Guide pour l'élaboration des politiques linguistiques éducatives en Europe, de la diversité linguistique à l'éducation plurilingue*, Beacco Jean-Claude, Byram Michael, Language Policy Division, Council of Europe, Strasbourg, version 1 (revised), 2003. page 72.

which is connected to educating citizens in the collective values of democratic conviviality.][45]

The citations given above – in which the spelling "*convivence*" is used – come from texts that pre-date the Académie Française's decision to approve the spelling "*conviv**a**nce*".

The spelling ending in "-**a**nce" was certainly also in use prior to the Académie Française's decision, and not just in the "Charte de la Convivance" issued by Pro Europae Unitatae. One such example can be found in a work by Bernard Vincent about Al-Andalus, published in spring 1994:

"A Grenade, jusqu'à la fin du XVe siècle, les minorités juive et chrétienne ont vécu à l'ombre d'un Islam majoritaire et dominant mais néanmoins protecteur.[46] Cette "*conviv**an**ce*" qui a permis aux trois communautés de vivre ensemble et a attiré à Grenade de nombreux réfugiés, cessa brutalement en 1492 avec le décret d'expulsion des juifs prononcé par les Rois

---

[45] Idem.

[46] Islam was both a dominant and protective religion in the sense that non-Muslim communities were forced to accept pacts that gave them certain economic, cultural and religious freedoms and guarantees in exchange for loyalty to the authorities and payment of additional taxes. These pacts worked in the Muslims' favour and were consistent with the principles of the Qu'ran (affording "dhimmi" – protected subject – status).

catholiques, qui sera suivi, dix ans plus tard, par le décret d'expulsion des musulmans." [Until the end of the 15th century, the Jewish and Christian minorities in Granada lived in the shadow of a dominant Muslim majority, yet this majority offered them protection. This convivence, which enabled the three communities to live together in peace and attracted a high number of refugees to Granada, came to a sudden end in 1492 when the Catholic Kings ordered the expulsion of the Jews and, ten years later, the expulsion of the Muslims.][47]

Armand Erchadi, who works on the *Dictionnaire de l'Académie Française*, conducted similar research in parallel to mine. The oldest occurrence of the word *convivance* that he was able to find was in a report by representatives Jean Debry and Charles Cochon to the Convention Nationale, on 9 February 1793. Requesting the replacement of Gasparin, who had fallen ill in Roye, with Carnot, they stated their reason as "un motif [de] *convivance* qui doit être compté pour quelque chose" [for the sake of convivence, which must count for something] *(French Parliamentary archives).*[48] The meaning of the word *convivance* in this instance remains unclear.

Armand Erchardi also had the following to say about the spelling "-ance":

---

[47] In *Confluences Méditérranéennes* no 10, 1994.

P. 51

[48] Armand Erchadi in a message...

"Henri Pichon spelled the word with an *a* in his work entitled *Vocabulaire de psychologie,* in which he cited neuropsychiatrist Jeroni de Moragas (1957); here the meaning of the word was a genuine state of community between coexisting peoples. In an article published in 1937, entitled "Exister avec le peuple", philosopher Jacques Maritain used the word in relation to ethics and morals, talking of "vivre en *convivance* morale avec [quelqu'un]" [living in moral convivence with [someone]]. Sociologist Gabriel Tarde, meanwhile, also used the *a* spelling in his work *L'Opposition universelle. Essai d'une théorie des contraires* (1897): "La concurrence est liée à la convivance." ["Competition is linked to convivence"].[49]

The Académie Française did not consider these precedents when making its decision. According to Florence Delay, the word *convivance* comes from the Old French verb "convivre" [to live together].

The decision to use the spelling "-**a**nce" therefore made sense, as "les formes en *-ant/-ance* dérivent plutôt de formes verbales (c'est le cas de *survivance*), alors que les formes en *-ent/-ence* ne sont pas toujours liées à un verbe." [the majority of words ending in "-ant/-ance" are verbal forms (such as "survivance", meaning "survival"), whereas words ending in "-ent/-ence" are not necessarily related to a verb].[50] and [51]

[49] Idem.
[50] Idem.

Another question raised is whether the word *convivance* is actually a neologism. It is a question of purity, and one that has caused a stir among defenders of the French language. Writer and journalist François Taillandier, for example, gave this reaction in a piece in *Le Figaro* in 2008 (he was a candidate for election to the Académie Française at the time[52]):

"Nous assimilons sans nous en douter une néo langue qui déconcerterait nos grands-parents [...] que diraient-ils devant le buzz et le capital osseux, le no-K-pote et la convivance, le people ready et le plan-tous-chez-moi?" [We are sleepwalking towards a neo-language that would leave our grandparents utterly bewildered [...] how on earth would they react to words such as "*buzz*"

---

[51] At the time of writing, the word *convivance* has still not been included in the Dictionnaire de l'Académie Française. It can, however, be found in the 2012 edition of the Dictionnaire Larousse, which gives the following definition: "Capacité de groupes humains différents à cohabiter harmonieusement au sein d'une entité locale, nationale, fédérale, communautaire etc." [The ability of different human groups to live together in harmony within the same local, national, federal or community entity.]

[52] He subsequently lost to another candidate in March 2009. Source: http://fr.wikipedia.org/wiki/François_Taillandier

and "*capital osseux*", "*no-K-pote*" and "*convivance*", "*people ready*" and "*plan-tous-chez-moi*"?][53]

In the opinion of Taillandier and others like him, "*convivance*" is therefore a neologism.

In Occitan, however, the word is definitely <u>not</u> a neologism:

"Ce mot, qui n'est pas un néologisme (...) Pourtant il est très à la mode. En effet, Abdelwahab Meddeb[54] l'utilise à plusieurs reprises dans son article paru dans Le Monde du 12 septembre dernier (2008) à propos de la visite du pape en France et intitulé "Pour une religion de la paix perpétuelle", qu'une phrase mise en exergue résume ainsi : "Finalement tous les humains ont une seule et même religion dont les formules et les cérémonies divergent ". (...) *Convivance* vient du mot occitan *convivencia*." [This word is not a neologism (...) It

---

[53] *Ce monde-là, Dictionnaire personnel de l'époque*, François Taillandier, Flammarion, 176 pages. Date unspecified. Discussed in *Le Figaro Magazine*, February 2008. <u>http://www.lefigaro.fr/lefigaromagazine/2008/02/09/01006-20080209ARTFIG00519-taillandier-l-incorrect.php</u>. Then see *La Langue Française au Défi*, Flammarion, September 2009. 100 pages. François Taillandier, was born in 1955 in Clermont-Ferrand. He is a French writer.

[54] Director of the international, cross-disciplinary journal *Dédale*, and tutor in comparative literature at Université Paris-X. At the time, he was also in charge of the weekly radio show *Cultures d'islam* on France Culture.

is, however widely used today. Indeed, Abdelwahab Meddeb used it several times in his article in *Le Monde* on 12 September 2008 when talking about the Pope's visit to France, entitled "Towards a religion of eternal peace", in which he stated that "In the end, all humans follow the same religion, it is only the details and ceremonies that differ (...) *Convivance* comes from the Occitan word *convivencia*."][55]

So who is right? While the Académie Française's thesaurus lists the word *convivance* as a neologism, it is not a *de facto* neologism, as our research, and that conducted by Echardi, show that it was in use well before 2004. In Occitan, meanwhile, the word *convivencia* seems to have existed for many centuries. The word *convivance* is also used when modern French is spoken in Occitania, as the following example about the Institut Occitania Al Andalus demonstrates:

"La vocation de l'Institut est de valoriser" le "patrimoine de *convivance* civilisationnelle, par des initiatives : conférences, séminaires, voyages d'études, publications, site internet, réseau..., pour le rendre plus accessible au grand public." [The Institute's aim is to promote and foster the convivence passed down to us from past civilisations, through initiatives such as conferences, seminars, study trips, publications, a website

---

[55] Source: *Le Monde*, 16 September 2008. Cited without reference on the following website: http://www.convivance-liens.com/Mona/articles.php?lng=fpg=104.

and a network, reaching as wide an audience as possible.][56]

The aims of this institute shed light on the development of the concept of *convivance* in France, particularly in response to the challenges that Europe is currently facing:

"Rappeler la mémoire et l'héritage culturel euro-méditerranéen, africain et transpyrénéen d'Al Andalus, pour mieux comprendre les enjeux cruciaux de l'Europe interculturelle d'aujourd'hui. Cet héritage arabo andalou dans ses relations avec l'Occitanie se perpétue plus que jamais de nos jours dans les formes nouvelles de mixité musicales, culturelles et spirituelles... [To promote the collective memory and European-Mediterranean, African and trans-Pyrenean cultural heritage of Al-Andalus as a response to the major intercultural challenges facing Europe today. The relationship forged between Arab Andalusia and Occitania resonates now more than ever in new forms of interaction between cultures in the fields of music, culture and spiritual matters...]

(...)

Contribuer à sensibiliser et former des hommes et des femmes, à une "civilité interculturelle", favoriser le rôle des migrants comme "passeurs interculturels". [To raise awareness and educate people in "intercultural

56 http://www.ostaldoccitania.net/articles.php?pg=900&lng=fr

civility", and to promote the importance of migrants as agents of "cultural transfer".]

Réinventer des liens et des échanges là où se creusent des ruptures, témoigner du vivier extraordinaire d'initiatives locales et transrégionales qui ouvrent des espérances et des futurs possibles. Relayer et s'associer à ceux qui construisent les passerelles et les ponts de paix et de fraternité entre les civilisations." [To reinvent relationships and interaction wherever change is occurring, and to promote the wealth of local and trans-regional initiatives that give hope for the future. To support and work alongside those who build bridges and pathways to peace and harmony between civilisations.][57]

Since 2004, the number of organisations, festivals and exhibitions on the topic of *convivance* has been on the rise in France. Examples can be found online, particularly on YouTube. This is a fast-growing trend and we have deliberately avoided citing any specific examples here, to avoid providing information that would be redundant at the time of reading.

---

[57] Idem

IV. The equivalent of *convivencia* in English: "convivence" and other expressions

The English language does not have a language standard-setting authority similar to the Académie Française or the Real Academia Española. In English, the acceptance of a particular word is inferred from its popularity and usage. English-speaking populations choose whether or not to adopt a given word and, when a term enters common usage, it is normally then included in the Oxford or Cambridge dictionary. At the time of writing, the word "convivence" could not be found in either of these dictionaries, nor was it included in the Merriam and Webster dictionary. Any attempt to assess the frequency with which the word "convivence" is used in the English-speaking world therefore involves looking at its usage rather than studying dictionaries.

In general, the words most commonly used at present with reference to the Al-Andalus period are "coexistence" and "cohabitation".

Below is an example of both of these words in use. The text is an extract from a conference paper given on 12 July 2012 by Professor Ramin Jahanbegloo, in which he discusses the time of Al-Andalus and the Caliphate of Córdoba:

"Cultural coexistence of this kind was made possible by religious and legal principles that were far-reaching in their implications. That is why the Andalusian experience is an exceptional moment in history, probably unique in its own time and rarely matched in any other.

The most notable and creative nature of the 'Cordoba paradigm' is that cohabitation and coexistence which were based on religious and legal principles." [58]

Another interesting example can be found in the title of an Ibero-American pedagogical work: "Hacia una Pedagogía de la Convivencia" [59] which has been translated into English as "Towards a Pedagogy of 'Coexistence'", i.e. not "of 'Convivence'".

There are also many examples of direct borrowing from Spanish:

The American website Websters Online Dictionary[60] with Multilingual Translation Thesaurus includes an entry for the word "*convivencia*", but none for "convivence". It does not give a direct definition of *convivencia*, instead explaining it as follows:

---

[58] *'The Cordoba Paradigm and the Cross-Cultural Learning'*. Conference paper given by Professeur Amin Jahanbegloo, 12 July 2012.

[59] Article 'Hacia una Pedagogía de la Convivencia' Roberto Arístegui, Domingo Bazán, Jorge Leiva, Ricardo López, Bernardo Muñoz y Juan Ruz, Organización de Estados Iberoamericanos (OEI), *PSYKHE* 2005, Vol. 14, N° 1, 137 – 150. http://www.scielo.cl/scielo.php?pid=S0718-22282005000100011&script=sci_arttext

[60] http://www.websters-online-dictionary.org/

"La **Convivencia** ("the Coexistence") is a term used to describe the situation in Spanish history from about 711 to 1492 (roughly concurrent with the Reconquista ("Reconquest"), when Jews, Muslims, and Catholics in Spain lived in relative peace together within the different kingdoms (…). The phrase often refers to the interplay of cultural ideas between the three groups, and ideas of religious tolerance".[61]

The title of a remarkable compilation of essays on the theme of *convivencia* in the time of Al-Andalus also uses the word *convivencia* in English:

Convivencia, Jews, Muslims and Christians in Medieval Spain Edited by Vivan B. Mann, Thomas F. Glick and Jerrilynn D. Dodds[62]. (See footnote on page 1).

Below are two other examples:

---

[61] http://www.websters-online-dictionary.org/definitions/convivencia. This professional and well-regarded website provides extremely accurate and detailed references from long-standing, authoritative British dictionaries. This level of detail is indicative of specialist, thorough research.

[62] *Convivencia, Jews, Muslims and Christians in Medieval Spain* Edited by Vivan B. Mann, Thomas F. Glick and Jerrilynn D. Dodds, George Braziller in association with The Jewish Museum, New York, (1992)

"A long period of "convivencia"-- living together -- and then 400+ years of religious and ethnic atrocities followed civil war and Franco's tyranny."[63]

and

"Islamic Spain has been hailed for its 'convivencia' — its spirit of tolerance in which Jews, Christians, and Muslims, created a premodern renaissance, Edward Rothstein writes in the New York Times." [64]

In both of these citations, there appears to be a certain embarrassment at the inability to clearly define the word *convivencia* in English. All of the suggested "equivalents" do, of course, form part of the concept of *convivencia* (in English, "convivence"), except perhaps the idea of "living in togetherness". The difference between "convivence" and "living in togetherness" is that "convivence" – through its semantic equivalence to "*convivencia*" – implies a link with the Al-Andalus civilisation, whereas this is not the case with "living in togetherness".

The word "*convivence*" first made an appearance in written English with reference to the need for dialogue

[63] Oriental Dreams, reference unclear, cited at http://www.wordnik.com/words/convivencia

[64] Edward Rothstein, New York Times, Philocrites, September 2003 Archives, reference unclear, cited at http://www.wordnik.com/words/convivencia

between religious communities. (We are not talking here about inter-cultural dialogue, but inter-religious dialogue only - although of course the majority of cultures are derived from religious sources.)

In a well-researched article entitled *Living with religious plurality*[65], Christoffer H. Grundmann details his research into the usage of the words "*convivence*" and "*convivencia*" in the English-speaking world, with reference to religious plurality. He reaches the following conclusion:

"What has nowadays become a concern for nearly everyone has actually always been such for the souvereigns [sic] of multicultural empires (...). One only need to think of Medieval Spain where Jews, Christians and Muslims lived fairly peacefully together... a situation that the historian Americo Castro (1885-1972) described as *convivencia*, a term rendered into English as living togetherness [sic]. (Castro[66], 1949 ;1971). By now,

---

[65] Christoffer H. Grundmann, Living with religious plurality, Some basic theological reflexions on Interreligious Dialogue. Valparaiso University. 2009. p. 133

[66] Castro, Américo, *Espana en su historica, cristianos, moros y judio*. Buenos Aires, Editorial Losada, Published in English in 1971 as The Spainards, An Introduction to their history. Enlarged by three chapters, Berkeley, University of California Press.

convivencia or convivence has become an accepted neologism in the English language… " [67]

Another author, Simon Benjamin, discusses the origin of the word *convivence* and its usage in an ecumenical context:

" …. The term convivence (living in togetherness) was borrowed by Sundermeier[68] from the South American liberation theology of Brazil.[69] Then it has found increasing use and denotes ‘a life actually lived with enthusiasm, encompassing experience and praxis, the individual and the collective, participation and exchange.’ Although the concept of *convivence* was originally mainly utilised for the [sic] dialogue between the religions,

---

[67] Grundmann's study was intended to show how the words "convivence" and "convivencia" have been widely used in the English-speaking world to refer to different religious communities living together in the same space, as well as in ecumenical research.

[68] ‘Das Evangelium leben in Südafrika’. In: Becker, Dieter (ed): ‘Mit dem Fremden leben: Perspektiven einer Theologie der Konvivenz': Theo Sundermeier zum 65 Geburtstag. Band 1: Religionen - Regionen. Missionswissenschaftliche Forschungen, Neue Folge, vol 11. Erlangen: Erlanger Verlag für Mission und Ökumene. 2000

[69] This begs the following question: if the word originally came from Brazil, can its origins be found in Portuguese?

initially Sundermeier also experimented with its use in oecumenic [sic] convivence.[70]"

The roots of the word "convivence" in the English language may therefore be found in the field of inter-religious dialogue. Having taken root in this way, the word then began to spread to other fields: Ikeaqwuchi Agbara, the English-speaking author of *The Possibility of Convivence in Nigeria: Towards Intercultural Hermeneutics and Religion in Dialogue*[71] suggests "*convivence*" as a model and method for a solution to the conflict in Nigeria. The author explains what the model involves as follows:

"The basic assumption (...) is that ethnic and religious pluralism have led to conflicts, but that they are fuelled by politics, inequitable distribution of economic goods and the negative forces of globalization. In this project, examining these conflicts and the efforts made to resolve them, particular attention will be paid to dialogue and reconciliation. The key practice suggested is

---

[70] Extract from Simon Benjamin, *From Migrants to Missionaries: Christians of African Origin in Germany, Studies in the intercultural History of Christianity*, Peter Lang, February 2010, 237 pages, page 215. This book is of particular interest as it looks for ways for the Roman Catholic Church to engage in ecumenical dialogue on a conceptual and theological level.

[71] Ikeaqwuchi Agbara, *The Possibility of Convivence in Nigeria: Towards Intercultural Hermeneutics and Religion in Dialogue*. LIT Verlag 2011, 224 pages

convivence: a symbiosis of interactive and interpenetrative approaches, based on intercultural and interreligious hermeneutical perspectives."[72]

Ikeaqwuchi Agbara borrows the term and its definition from Thomas Glick in *Convivencia, Jews, Muslims and Christians in Medieval Spain.* (See note 62.)

Translators have played a major role in the introduction of the words *convivencia* and *convivence* into English vocabulary. Numerous examples of this work in practice can be seen on translators' support sites and forums. Our research suggests that, when the word *convivencia* is part of a document title (such as the *Certificado de Convivencia*), then *convivencia* is retained in the English translation. However, when translators are working on Spanish texts and are required to translate the concepts underlying *convivencia* into English – i.e. coexistence, inter-cultural dialogue, the problems surrounding the cohabitation of individuals or groups – they tend to prefer the words "coexistence", "cohabitation" and even "living in togetherness".

We have deliberately excluded any specific references here, as online websites and forums are constantly changing.

In general, the word "convivence" is more widely used in the United States than in the United Kingdom.

---

[72] Book Description from Amazon. http://www.amazon.com/Possibility-Convivence-Nigeria-Religionspadagogik-interkulturell/dp/3643800916

The subtle influence of Latin American appears to be a contributing factor to the growing popularity of this expression.

Here are some examples of the word "convivence" used in spoken language, taken from small (and by definition temporary) online adverts: a Mexican babysitter looking for work who lists "good convivence" as one of her qualities; a hotel promoting its excellent social facilities, student club, etc. uses the word "convivence" to describe the warm, welcoming and friendly atmosphere within the establishment. [73] It may therefore be argued that the word "convivence" is gaining ground in common usage.

---

[73] These adverts are only online for a short period of time, so there is no value in providing references.

V. Does the word *convivencia* have any synonyms?

In this section, we will compare the words *convivencia*, *convivance* and “convivence” with similar words:

Why do we need the word *convivencia* (*convivance*, “convivence”)?

The concept that underlies these words is similar to the idea of "conviviality" and "community", but is not limited to these meanings:

The 1987 edition of the Hachette *Dictionnaire de la langue française* gave the following definition of "convivialité": "goût pour les repas réunissant de nombreux convives. → Par extension : ensemble des rapports de tolérance et d’échange entre des personnes ou des groupes appartenant à la même société".[74] Et d’ajouter : "en anglais, conviviality".[75] [a preference for dining with multiple guests → By extension: referring to tolerance and exchanges between individuals or groups belonging to the same society. In English: "conviviality".]

"Coexistence", meanwhile, refers to a situation in which different individuals or groups of living organisms share the same space. Where the meaning is derived from Latin, it may refer to a static situation in which exchange

---

[74] *Dictionnaire de la Langue française*. 40,000 definitions. Hachette. 1987.

[75] Idem. 1987 version, p. 242

is not required or not necessarily sought. It also has links to the Cold War period and the concept of "peaceful coexistence". In this sense, its meaning is too restrictive and cannot be applied to the situation in Córdoba, where exchange was actively sought and individuals and groups made deliberate contact with others. The term *convivencia, convivance, convivence*, however, does indeed imply coexistence: in order for "*convivencia*" (and its French and English equivalents) to exist, there must necessarily be at least two entities within the same space or area.

Anne Françoise Weber, French author of a work about mixed couples (marriages between Muslims and Christians) in Lebanon, explains her decision to the use the word *convivance* (on page 14 of her book) as follows: "afin de palier aux carences des termes '*coexistence*', qui ne dit rien sur la 'qualité des relations' et *convivialité* qui évoque un '*état de la société'* plutôt que '*l'action de vivre ensemble*' ". [to overcome the insufficiencies of the terms "coexistence", which provides no information about the "quality of relationships", and "conviviality", which suggests "the existence of a community" rather than the "action of living together."][76]

---

[76] According to Samer Mitri, who reviewed this book in the journal *Les Clés du Moyen Orient* *http://www.lesclesdumoyenorient.com/Anne-Francoise-Weber-Le-Cedre.html.* Review date not provided. The book in question is Anne Françoise Weber's *Le Cèdre*

The terms *convivencia*, *convivance* and "convivence", imply both "conviviality" and "coexistence", but cannot be reduced to these concepts alone.

The word "cohabitation", meanwhile, refers to individuals or groups living together in the same location, or to parties in government. The word *convivencia* may, of course, be used to signify cohabitation. The *Registro Civil* of both Buenos Aires and Murcia, for example, issues people who need to prove that they live in the same location with a "*Certificado de convivencia*."[77] However "cohabitation" is, again, only one element of the broader concept of *convivencia*.

What about the word "tolerance"? The term implies effort to accept things that would not normally be accepted, and in some cases involves overcoming an existing state of contempt or rejection. In this case too, tolerance is part of the wider conceptual field of *convivencia*.

This exercise can be repeated with other words, in an attempt to find a direct synonym for *convivencia*. However, all possible candidates are more limited in scope than *convivencia* and, while they form part of the broader definition of the word, they do not fully represent

---

islamo chrétien : Des Libanais à la recherche de l'unité nationale. Baden Baden, Nomos, 2007.

77 http://forum.wordreference.com/showthread.php?t=2024700

its entire meaning. There is perhaps on exception to this rule, found in the English expression "living in togetherness". However this term contains no implicit reference to *convivencia* in Córdoba and Al-Andalus.

Conclusion

The word *convivencia* was not in use in Córdoba at the time of the Umayyad Caliphate, or during the Al-Andalus period. However, the legal concept of "*convivencia*" was applied by Muslims from the time of the Iberian Peninsula invasion in the 8th century AD.

The word *convivencia* is a neologism and it is difficult to ascertain the precise moment at which its Spanish, French and English versions entered common usage. However, the concept of "*convivencia*" has existed – and has evolved – since the period of Al-Andalus and Córdoba.

Today, it is used to refer to attempts to create harmony between individuals and populations living in the same area. The word *convivencia* is widely used in Spanish, as is the word *convivance* in French. The words *convivencia* and "convivence" are both gaining ground in British English.

A comparison of the words *convivencia*, *convivance* and "convivence" (in Spanish, French and English respectively) with other terms such as "coexistence", "tolerance" and "cohabitation" (and their Spanish and French equivalents) suggests that there are no synonyms for this term.

Dominique-D Junod (Arbell)

PhD Political Sciences. Ancient and Modern Studies's Mastery. University of Geneva.

October 2012

Book realised by Florent Huet.
Printed in March 2015 by
Lulu Enterprises, Inc., Raleigh, N.C.
on behalf of
Florent Huet, 5 ter rue de Verdun, 54800 Jeandelize.
Legal Deposit: April 2015

www.ingramcontent.com/pod-product-compliance
Ingram Content Group UK Ltd.
Pitfield, Milton Keynes, MK11 3LW, UK
UKHW021642190726
13853UKWH00001B/10

9 791091 662215